Thinking

A Troll Question Book™

By Kathie Billingslea Smith & Victoria Crenson
Illustrated by Robert S. Storms
Medical Consultant: Ira T. Fine, M.D.

Library of Congress Cataloging in Publication Data

Smith, Kathie Billingslea.
Thinking.

(A Troll question book)
Summary: Uses a question and answer format to explain
such things as how our brain works to let us think,
learn, and feel emotions, what happens when we sleep,
and what brain damage is.
1. Brain—Juvenile literature.   2. Thought and
thinking—Juvenile literature.   3. Cognition—Juvenile
literature.   [1. Brain.   2. Thought and thinking.
3. Questions and answers]   I. Crenson, Victoria.
II. Storms, Robert S., ill.   III. Title.
QP376.S643   1988   612'.82   87-5886
ISBN 0-8167-1016-3 (lib. bdg.)
ISBN 0-8167-1017-1 (pbk.)

Troll Associates
Mahwah, N.J.

Your brain is the "big boss" of your body. It lets you think, feel emotions, breathe, remember, talk, and move. You need your brain even to blink an eye. It tells you when you are hungry or thirsty, when something is funny or sad, and how to count. Every minute of the day and night, whether you are awake or asleep, your brain is busy.

Some people have compared the brain to a computer. Like a computer, the brain collects information and stores it in its memory. Then it pulls out and uses the information to keep the body machinery running smoothly. But the brain is much better than a computer. A computer cannot laugh, cry, wish, or love.

my brain?

Your brain is what makes you special — different from anyone else. You have your own thoughts, ideas, memories, and feelings.

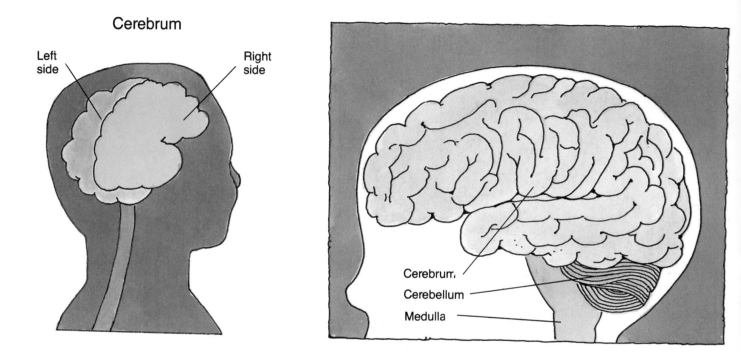

Cerebrum

Left side

Right side

Cerebrum
Cerebellum
Medulla

Your brain looks a bit like a large, wrinkled walnut. It is gray on the outside and white on the inside. It is made up of billions of nerve cells.

The brain has three main parts. Each part deals with a different activity.

The largest part is the *cerebrum*. It is divided into two halves. The cerebrum controls thinking, imagination, memory, and feelings. It also directs any movements that you decide to make with your body. The left half of the cerebrum controls the right side of your body. And the right half controls the left side.

# of my brain?

Breathing

Balance

Underneath the cerebrum is the *cerebellum*. This part of the brain controls balance.

The brain stem, or *medulla*, is at the top of the spinal column.

It takes care of important body actions that you don't even have to think about — like breathing, digestion, and heartbeat. Your medulla is always working to keep you alive.

How big is my brain?

Use your hands to feel the outside of your head. Press against your forehead. Touch the sides of your head. Then feel the top and back of your head, down to the neck. All of this space is filled with your brain.

Have you ever seen one of your baby pictures? Your head probably looked very big compared to your tiny body.

Although a newborn baby's brain weighs less than one pound, it already has billions of nerve cells so that the baby can begin learning. The brain builds connections between its cells as the baby experiences new things. During the first six years, the brain grows very rapidly. By age fifteen, the brain is full-grown.

If you could weigh your brain now, you would find out that it weighs about three pounds!

Scientists have discovered that a bigger brain does not make someone smarter. The brains of smart people have more wrinkles.

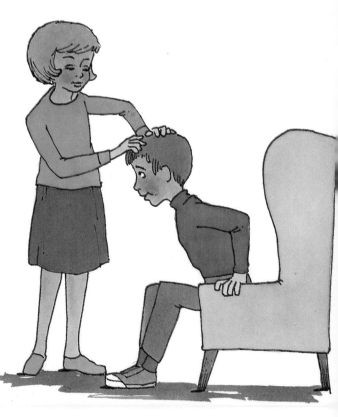

13 oz.

Baby

2 lbs.

One-year-old

2 lbs.
3 oz.

Two-
year-old

2 lbs.
7 oz.

Three-year-old

2 lbs.
11 oz.

Four-year-old

2 lbs.
14 oz.

Six-year-old

All your muscles and organs are "wired" to the brain by a network of nerve cells. Eyes, ears, nose, tongue, and skin send coded messages to the brain. The brain decodes the information. Then it sends messages back telling your body what to do.

Some of the information the brain receives is stored away in the cerebrum as memories. The cerebrum contains billions of tiny nerve cells all linked together. These connections let you think thoughts, make decisions, and discover new ideas.

think?

Scientists still do not understand completely how the brain works, but they do know that information passes between nerve cells as a spark of electricity!

When you learn something new, the brain cells in your cerebrum work together to help you understand and remember.

Suppose you meet a new boy in the neighborhood. Your eyes send a message to your brain telling what he looks like. You hear him say that his name is

learn?

Kevin, and your ears send that information on to the brain. Very quickly your brain compares that new boy to other friends. It tells you that he is someone you have not met before. Your brain stores Kevin's name and an image of him. From then on, whenever you see Kevin or hear his name, your brain uses these stored images to tell you who he is.

Why can I r m mber som

Messages are constantly being sent to your brain. You remember what seems important. But you can't remember everything. Much of what you see, hear, or feel is soon forgotten.

The brain divides the information it receives into short-term and long-term memory. Short-term memory only keeps a thought for a minute or so. Then it is forgotten. But, by paying special attention, the brain can make a thought part of your long-term memory.

things but not others?

Often you remember what you have seen or heard many times. You remember your phone number because it's important. It's become part of your long-term memory.

Your brain is full of memories. Every day you add new ones. Maybe today you learned a new song, heard a story, or discovered a special climbing tree.

What does my brain do

Zzzzzzz.

When you are asleep, your body relaxes and slows down. Your eyes and ears and other senses rest. They do not send very many messages to your brain. This allows part of the brain — the cerebrum — to relax, too. While the brain is relaxed, it often begins to dream.

wnen I'm asleep?

Some dreams are funny. Some are fanciful. Others are scary. Everybody has these dreams.

Scientists do not understand very much about dreams. But they do know that dreaming is good for you. When you dream, you can think of ideas and feelings in new ways. You can be in an imaginary world where things don't happen as they do in real life.

At different times each day, you may feel happy or sad or surprised or scared or angry. We all have different emotions and feelings.

These feelings begin deep inside the cerebrum in a part called the *limbic system*. You cannot control these feelings, but how you handle them can be controlled.

differ nt feelings?

If you are very angry at a person, you may want to hit that person or say something mean. But the thinking part of your brain might tell you a better way to handle the situation. You could talk it over with the person or simply walk away.

As you grow older, you learn new ways to deal with your feelings.

What is brain damage?

Some people have brains that are damaged due to accidents, diseases, infections, strokes, or birth defects.

If the part of the brain that directs body movement is damaged, then the person will not be able to control his or her arms and legs. People with cerebral palsy have this problem. They may use motorized wheelchairs to get around, but they can think very well!

If the nerve cells carrying information from the eyes or ears to the brain are damaged, a person may be blind or deaf.

When the part of the brain that deals with thinking is hurt, a person has difficulty learning. He or she has to work hard to learn what may seem easy for you. There may be some things that person can never learn to do.

But there is one thing we can *all* do . . . have fun!

Do animals think th

Most animals have brains that are suited to the kinds of lives they lead. Insects' brains are just small groups of nerves. The brains do not control what the insects do. Grasshoppers that have had their brains removed can still walk and jump!

Chimpanzees and gorillas are the smartest animals — next to people. Some of them have even been taught to "speak" using sign language! One famous gorilla named Koko lets people know that she is "fine animal gorilla."

Birds, too, have well-developed brains. They use them to find food and to balance in the air as they fly. Birds can be taught to do many tricks. Scientists have taught some pigeons to look at a group of objects and pick out the one that is different from the others!

Another very smart animal is the dolphin. Scientists think dolphins have their own language. They talk to each other with clicks and squeaks. These very playful animals can be taught to do difficult tricks. Some swimmers have even been saved from drowning by helpful dolphins.

Elephants and whales have brains that are bigger than ours. But their bodies are a lot bigger, too.

Compared to the size of our bodies, human brains are giant-sized! No other animal can talk, listen, and learn the way we can.

Your brain is protected by a hard, bony covering called the *skull*. It helps to shield the brain from bumps or blows to the head. But even with a built-in protector, the brain still needs to be treated very carefully.

When playing sports such as baseball, hockey, or football, always wear the proper equipment to protect your head. It is also a good idea to wear a biking helmet when cycling.

If you ever hurt your head, go to a doctor or hospital at once. A

The skull

# of my brain?

bad head injury can destroy many brain cells.

Try to get enough sleep each night. Your brain works best when you are relaxed and rested.

How can I learn more?

Have you ever wanted to learn how to ice skate or type or speak Spanish or play the guitar?

If you concentrate and try hard enough, you can probably learn to do almost anything!

The brain has great potential. Most people never use more than a fraction of their brain power. But the more you use your brain, the smarter you will be! Your brain will never get too full of thoughts and ideas.

What more would you like to learn?